Mastering Your Finances: A Guide to Budgeting

Corey Atkinson

Published by Corey Atkinson, 2023.

MASTERING YOUR FINANCES: A GUIDE TO BUDGETING

First edition. May 22, 2023.

ISBN: 979-8223578475

Written by Corey Atkinson.

Title: Mastering Your Finances: A Guide to Budgeting

Introduction:

Welcome to "Mastering Your Finances," a comprehensive guide to taking control of your financial life and achieving long-term success. In the pages ahead, you will embark on a transformative journey that will empower you to make informed decisions, set achievable goals, and ultimately build a secure and prosperous future.

Money plays a vital role in our lives. It influences the choices we make, the opportunities we pursue, and the lifestyles we lead. Yet, despite its significance, many people struggle with managing their finances effectively. Whether it's living pay-check to pay-check, drowning in debt, or feeling overwhelmed by complex investment options, the challenges can seem insurmountable.

But fear not! This book is designed to equip you with the knowledge, strategies, and tools necessary to navigate the intricacies of personal finance with confidence and clarity. Whether you're a recent graduate starting your financial journey or a seasoned professional seeking to optimize your wealth, the principles outlined here are universally applicable and adaptable to your unique circumstances.

Throughout the chapters, we will explore various aspects of personal finance, including budgeting, saving, investing, debt management, and retirement planning. Each topic will be demystified, breaking down complex concepts into accessible, actionable steps. Along the way, we'll provide real-world examples, practical tips, and expert insights to help you make informed decisions.

It's essential to recognize that mastering your finances is not just about accumulating wealth for its own sake. It's about gaining control over your financial life, so you can live the life you desire. It's about aligning your money with your values and priorities, fostering financial security, and building a solid foundation for your dreams and aspirations.

While there's no one-size-fits-all approach to personal finance, this book will provide you with a framework that can be customized to suit your circumstances and goals. We encourage you to take an active role in your financial journey, ask questions, and engage with the content. Remember, your financial well-being is within your grasp, and the decisions you make today will shape your future.

So, let's embark on this transformative journey together. By the time you reach the final page, you will have the knowledge, skills, and confidence to master your finances and build a prosperous future. Get ready to unlock your financial potential and embark on a lifetime of financial well-being. The journey starts now.

Chapter 1: Understanding Budgeting

Importance of Budgeting

Budgeting is a crucial financial management tool that helps individuals, households, businesses, and organizations plan, allocate, and control their financial resources. Here are some key reasons why budgeting is important:

1. Financial Planning: Budgeting allows you to create a financial plan by setting goals, estimating income, and outlining expected expenses. It provides a roadmap for how you will manage your money, helping you prioritize your spending and saving.

2. Goal Achievement: A budget helps you work towards your short-term and long-term financial goals. Whether it's saving for a down payment on a house, paying off debt, starting a business, or planning for retirement, budgeting ensures that you allocate funds towards these objectives.

3. Expense Control: Budgeting enables you to track your expenses and gain a clear understanding of where your money is going. By identifying unnecessary or excessive spending, you can make informed decisions and cut back on non-essential items, thereby reducing financial waste.

4. Debt Management: A budget plays a vital role in managing and reducing debt. By allocating funds towards debt repayment, you can make consistent progress in paying off loans or credit card balances, avoid accumulating further debt, and ultimately improve your financial health.

5. Emergency Preparedness: Life is unpredictable, and unexpected expenses can arise. Having a budget allows you to set aside funds for emergencies, creating a safety net to handle unforeseen circumstances such as medical expenses, car repairs, or job loss without jeopardizing your financial stability.

6. Improved Decision Making: Budgeting provides a clear financial overview, enabling you to make informed decisions about spending,

saving, and investing. It helps you evaluate the feasibility of financial choices, compare alternatives, and make adjustments as needed.

7. Financial Awareness and Discipline: Budgeting cultivates financial discipline and encourages mindful spending. It promotes awareness of your financial situation, highlights areas for improvement, and encourages responsible financial habits.

8. Long-Term Wealth Building: By consistently following a budget, you can save and invest for the future, leading to long-term wealth accumulation and financial security. Budgeting allows you to allocate funds towards investments, retirement accounts, or other wealth-building opportunities.

Overall, budgeting empowers individuals and organizations to take control of their finances, make informed choices, and work towards their financial goals. It is a fundamental tool for achieving financial stability, reducing debt, and building wealth.

Benefits of Budgeting

Budgeting offers numerous benefits, both in personal and business contexts. Here are some key advantages of budgeting:

1. Financial Control: Budgeting gives you control over your finances by allowing you to track your income and expenses. It helps you understand where your money is going, identify areas of overspending, and make adjustments to ensure you are living within your means.

2. Goal Achievement: A budget helps you set and achieve financial goals. Whether it's saving for a vacation, paying off debt, or starting a business, budgeting enables you to allocate funds towards specific objectives, making them more attainable.

3. Debt Management: Budgeting plays a crucial role in managing and reducing debt. By creating a debt repayment plan within your budget, you can allocate extra funds towards paying off loans or credit card balances, accelerating your journey to becoming debt-free.

4. Improved Saving Habits: Budgeting encourages saving by setting aside a portion of your income for future needs and goals. It helps you prioritize saving and build an emergency fund, retirement savings, or funds for large purchases.

5. Decision Making: With a budget in place, you can make informed financial decisions. By having a clear understanding of your financial situation, you can evaluate the feasibility of purchases, investments, or other financial choices, and make decisions aligned with your overall financial goals.

6. Financial Awareness: Budgeting cultivates financial awareness by making you more conscious of your spending patterns and habits. It highlights areas where you may be overspending or wasting money, enabling you to make adjustments and develop more mindful spending habits.

7. Reduced Financial Stress: Having a budget can significantly reduce financial stress. It provides a sense of control and security, as

you have a clear plan for managing your money and handling expenses. By knowing where your money is going, you can make more confident financial decisions and alleviate anxiety about financial matters.

8. Improved Financial Relationships: Budgeting can positively impact relationships, whether personal or business. In personal relationships, it promotes financial transparency, teamwork, and shared financial goals. In business, budgeting helps allocate resources effectively, set performance targets, and make informed financial decisions.

9. Long-Term Financial Stability: By consistently following a budget, you can establish financial stability over time. Budgeting allows you to live within your means, save for the future, and build a solid foundation for long-term financial security.

10. Financial Freedom: Ultimately, budgeting can lead to financial freedom. It helps you achieve your financial goals, reduce debt, save for retirement, and build wealth. By effectively managing your money, you gain the freedom to make choices aligned with your values and aspirations.

These benefits highlight the transformative impact of budgeting on personal and financial well-being, providing a roadmap to achieve financial success and peace of mind.

Common Budgeting Misconceptions

There are several common misconceptions about budgeting that can hinder individuals from effectively managing their finances. Here are a few of them:

1. Budgeting is too restrictive: One common misconception is that budgeting restricts your financial freedom and limits your ability to enjoy life. However, a budget is simply a tool to help you allocate your money wisely and prioritize your spending based on your financial goals and values. A well-designed budget can actually provide a sense of control and empower you to make informed choices that align with your priorities.

2. Budgeting is only for people with financial problems: Another misconception is that budgeting is only necessary for individuals who are struggling financially. In reality, budgeting is beneficial for everyone, regardless of their income level. It helps individuals of all financial backgrounds manage their money effectively, achieve their goals, and build wealth. Budgeting is a proactive approach to financial management rather than a reactive solution to financial problems.

3. Budgeting is too time-consuming: Some people believe that budgeting requires a significant amount of time and effort, making it impractical for their busy lives. While creating a budget initially may require some time and effort, maintaining and updating it can be relatively simple. There are numerous budgeting tools and apps available that automate the process and make it more convenient and less time-consuming.

4. Budgeting means cutting back on everything: Budgeting does involve prioritizing your spending, but it doesn't necessarily mean eliminating all enjoyable or discretionary expenses. It's about finding a balance between your needs, wants, and financial goals. By understanding your spending patterns and making conscious choices,

you can identify areas where you can reduce expenses without sacrificing everything you enjoy.

5. Budgeting is inflexible: Some people view budgeting as a rigid framework that cannot accommodate unexpected expenses or changes in circumstances. However, a budget can be flexible and adaptable. It's essential to build some flexibility into your budget to account for unforeseen expenses or changes in income. Regularly reviewing and adjusting your budget allows you to adapt to changing circumstances while staying on track with your financial goals.

6. Budgeting is only about cutting expenses: While controlling expenses is an important aspect of budgeting, it's not the sole focus. Budgeting also involves maximizing your income, whether through salary negotiation, additional income streams, or investment opportunities. Increasing your income can provide more financial stability and support your long-term financial goals.

By dispelling these misconceptions, individuals can recognize the value and importance of budgeting as a powerful tool for financial management and achieving their desired financial outcomes.

Chapter 2: Assessing Your Financial Situation

Evaluating Your Income Sources

Evaluating income sources is a crucial step in understanding your overall financial picture and making informed decisions about budgeting, saving, and investing. Here are some steps to evaluate your income sources effectively:

1. Identify Your Primary Income Source: Determine your primary source of income, which is typically your main job or business. This income source forms the foundation of your financial situation and should be evaluated in terms of stability, growth potential, and satisfaction.

2. Calculate Net Income: Calculate your net income, which is the amount of money you take home after taxes, deductions, and other withholdings. Understanding your net income provides a realistic view of how much money you have available to allocate towards your financial goals.

3. Consider Additional Income Streams: Assess if you have any additional sources of income beyond your primary source. These could include part-time jobs, freelance work, rental income, dividends from investments, or interest from savings accounts. Evaluate the reliability and growth potential of these income streams.

4. Analyze Income Stability: Examine the stability of your income sources. Determine if your primary income source is secure or if there is a risk of job loss or significant fluctuations. Assess the stability of additional income streams as well. A diversified income portfolio can provide more stability and protect against unexpected income loss.

5. Project Income Growth Potential: Consider the growth potential of your income sources. Assess if there are opportunities for salary increases, promotions, or expanding your business. Evaluate the potential for passive income from investments or other ventures. Identifying income growth opportunities can help you plan for the future and set realistic financial goals.

6. Evaluate Non-Monetary Benefits: While financial considerations are important, also consider non-monetary benefits that come with your income sources. These could include healthcare benefits, retirement contributions, flexible work arrangements, or career development opportunities. These benefits contribute to your overall financial well-being and should be taken into account.

7. Regularly Review and Update: Income sources can change over time, so it's crucial to regularly review and update your evaluation. Stay informed about changes in your primary job, potential career opportunities, investment returns, or any new income streams that may arise. This ensures that your financial plans and budgeting efforts remain aligned with your current income situation.

By evaluating your income sources thoroughly, you gain a comprehensive understanding of your financial foundation, allowing you to make informed decisions, set realistic goals, and effectively manage your finances.

Identifying and Categorizing Expenses

Identifying and categorizing expenses is an essential step in budgeting and financial management. It helps you understand where your money is going, identify areas of overspending, and make informed decisions about allocating your funds. Here's a guide to identifying and categorizing expenses effectively:

1. Track Your Expenses: Start by tracking all your expenses for a certain period, such as a month. Keep a record of every purchase, payment, or expenditure you make. You can use mobile apps, spreadsheets, or even pen and paper to note down the details.

2. Group Similar Expenses: Once you have a comprehensive list of expenses, group them into broad categories. Common expense categories include housing, transportation, food, utilities, entertainment, healthcare, debt payments, savings, and miscellaneous expenses.

3. Create Specific Subcategories: Within each broad category, create more specific subcategories. For example, within the food category, you might have subcategories like groceries, dining out, and coffee shops. In the transportation category, you could have subcategories like fuel, public transportation, and car maintenance.

4. Review and Adjust: Review your expense categories and subcategories regularly to ensure they accurately reflect your spending habits and priorities. Adjust or add categories as needed to capture all relevant expenses and create a clear and meaningful breakdown of your spending.

5. Allocate Expenses to Categories: Assign each expense to its corresponding category and subcategory. This process may involve going through your recorded expenses and placing them in the appropriate categories based on their nature and purpose. Be diligent and accurate in categorizing each expense to gain an accurate understanding of your spending patterns.

6. Use Technology and Tools: Utilize budgeting tools, expense tracking apps, or personal finance software that can automatically categorize your expenses based on transaction details. These tools can streamline the categorization process and save you time and effort.

7. Analyze and Interpret the Data: Once you have categorized your expenses, analyze the data to gain insights into your spending habits. Look for trends, identify areas of overspending or potential savings, and assess how your expenses align with your financial goals.

8. Adjust Your Budget: Use the information from your categorized expenses to adjust your budget accordingly. Allocate appropriate amounts to each expense category, ensuring you have enough to cover essential needs while also prioritizing savings and financial goals.

9. Review and Maintain Regularly: Regularly review and update your expense categories as your spending patterns change over time. It's important to stay proactive and ensure that your budget accurately reflects your current financial situation.

By identifying and categorizing your expenses, you gain clarity and control over your financial life. This process allows you to make informed decisions, identify areas for improvement, and ensure that your spending aligns with your financial goals.

Analyzing Spending Patterns

Analyzing your spending patterns is an important step in understanding your financial habits, identifying areas for improvement, and making informed decisions about budgeting and saving. Here's a guide on how to effectively analyze your spending patterns:

1. Gather Your Financial Data: Collect all your financial records, including bank statements, credit card statements, receipts, and any other documentation that tracks your expenses. Make sure you have a comprehensive overview of your spending for a specific period, such as a month or a few months.

2. Categorize Your Expenses: Categorize your expenses into broad categories, such as housing, transportation, food, utilities, entertainment, healthcare, debt payments, savings, and miscellaneous expenses. Use the categories that you have created or follow pre-established budgeting categories.

3. Calculate Total Spending: Calculate the total amount you spent in each category for the selected period. Sum up the expenses within each category to get a clear picture of your overall spending distribution.

4. Compare Spending to Income: Compare your total spending to your total income for the same period. This will help you understand what percentage of your income you are spending and identify if you are living within your means or if adjustments need to be made.

5. Identify High-Cost Categories: Analyze which expense categories have the highest spending. These categories may indicate areas where you can potentially cut back or find ways to save money. For example, if you notice that your dining out expenses are high, you may consider reducing the frequency of eating out or finding more affordable alternatives.

6. Spot Trends and Patterns: Look for trends and patterns in your spending. Are there any specific months or seasons when your spending is higher or lower? Do you tend to overspend in certain categories during

certain times? Identifying these patterns can help you anticipate and plan for future expenses.

7. Assess Essential vs. Discretionary Spending: Differentiate between essential and discretionary expenses. Essential expenses are necessary for basic needs, such as housing, utilities, and food. Discretionary expenses are non-essential and include entertainment, shopping, and dining out. Evaluate if your spending aligns with your priorities and consider whether you can reallocate funds from discretionary expenses to savings or debt repayment.

8. Identify Opportunities for Savings: Look for areas where you can potentially reduce expenses and save money. Analyze if there are any recurring expenses that can be eliminated or reduced. This might involve renegotiating bills, finding more cost-effective alternatives, or cutting back on unnecessary purchases.

9. Set Realistic Budgeting Goals: Based on your spending analysis, set realistic budgeting goals. Determine how much you want to allocate to each expense category moving forward and establish a budget that aligns with your financial priorities and objectives.

10. Regularly Review and Adjust: It's crucial to regularly review and adjust your spending patterns as your financial situation and goals evolve. Continuously monitor your expenses, compare them to your budget, and make necessary adjustments to stay on track.

By analyzing your spending patterns, you gain valuable insights into your financial habits and can make informed decisions about budgeting, saving, and achieving your financial goals.

Chapter 3: Creating Your Budget

Setting Financial Goals

Setting financial goals is a critical step in creating a roadmap for your financial success. Well-defined goals provide clarity, motivation, and direction for your financial decisions and actions. Here's a guide on how to set effective financial goals:

1. Assess Your Current Financial Situation: Begin by evaluating your current financial situation. Take stock of your income, expenses, assets, debts, savings, and investments. Understand where you currently stand financially to set realistic and achievable goals.

2. Identify Short-Term and Long-Term Goals: Distinguish between short-term and long-term goals. Short-term goals typically span one year or less, while long-term goals extend beyond one year. Short-term goals can include building an emergency fund, paying off a credit card, or saving for a vacation. Long-term goals might include saving for retirement, buying a house, or funding a child's education.

3. Make Goals Specific and Measurable: Ensure that your goals are specific and measurable. Instead of setting a general goal like "save more money," specify an exact amount or percentage you want to save within a certain timeframe. Measurable goals allow you to track your progress and celebrate milestones along the way.

4. Prioritize Your Goals: Rank your goals based on importance and urgency. Determine which goals are most crucial to your financial well-being and prioritize them accordingly. This helps you allocate your resources and efforts effectively.

5. Set Realistic and Attainable Goals: It's essential to set goals that are realistic and attainable within your current financial situation. Consider factors such as your income, expenses, debts, and savings capacity. Setting unattainable goals can lead to frustration and demotivation. Start with smaller, achievable goals that can build momentum toward larger ones.

6. Break Goals Down into Actionable Steps: Break down each goal into actionable steps. Identify the specific actions or milestones needed to accomplish the goal. For example, if your goal is to pay off a debt, your action steps could include creating a budget, reducing discretionary spending, and allocating extra funds towards debt repayment each month.

7. Assign Timeframes to Goals: Establish timeframes for achieving your goals. Determine when you want to accomplish each goal and set deadlines for specific milestones along the way. Having timeframes helps create a sense of urgency and accountability.

8. Review and Adjust Regularly: Regularly review your goals and progress. Assess if any adjustments or modifications are needed based on changes in your financial situation or priorities. Adapt your goals as necessary to stay aligned with your evolving needs and circumstances.

9. Celebrate Milestones and Progress: Acknowledge and celebrate your achievements as you reach milestones along the way. Recognizing your progress provides motivation and reinforces positive financial habits.

10. Seek Professional Guidance if Needed: Consider seeking guidance from a financial advisor or planner, especially for complex or long-term goals like retirement planning or investment strategies. A financial professional can provide expert advice, help you develop a personalized plan, and ensure your goals are in line with your overall financial objectives.

By setting clear, realistic, and actionable financial goals, you can take control of your financial future and make intentional decisions that lead to long-term financial success and security.

Allocating Income To Essential Expenses

Allocating income to essential expenses is a crucial aspect of budgeting and financial management. It ensures that you cover your basic needs and obligations before allocating funds to other discretionary expenses. Here's a guide on how to effectively allocate your income to essential expenses:

1. Identify Essential Expenses: Start by identifying your essential expenses, which are necessary for your basic needs and obligations. These typically include:

- Housing: Rent or mortgage payments, property taxes, utilities, and home insurance.
- Food: Groceries, essential household supplies, and dining at home.
- Transportation: Vehicle loan or lease payments, fuel, insurance, maintenance, and public transportation costs.
- Utilities: Electricity, water, gas, and internet/phone bills.
- Debt Payments: Minimum payments on credit cards, loans, and any other outstanding debts.
- Insurance: Health insurance, life insurance, and other necessary coverage.
- Healthcare: Medical expenses, prescriptions, and regular check-ups.
- Education: Tuition fees, student loans, or other educational expenses if applicable.
- Personal Care: Basic toiletries and personal grooming items.

2. Determine the Total Cost: Calculate the total amount required to cover your essential expenses for a specific period, such as a month. Add up the costs of each category to get a clear understanding of the total amount needed.

3. Prioritize and Allocate Income: Prioritize your essential expenses by assigning them the highest priority in your budget. Allocate a portion of your income specifically to cover these expenses. Start by ensuring

that these essential expenses are fully funded before allocating money to discretionary expenses or savings.

4. Create a Budget: Use the total cost of your essential expenses as a foundation for creating a budget. Consider your income and allocate funds to each category accordingly. Ensure that the total allocated amount for essential expenses does not exceed your income.

5. Review and Adjust: Regularly review your essential expenses to ensure that they accurately reflect your needs and any changes in your financial situation. Adjust your budget as needed to accommodate any fluctuations in costs or income.

6. Seek Cost-Saving Opportunities: Look for ways to reduce costs within your essential expenses. This could involve finding more affordable housing options, exploring discounts on utilities, shopping wisely for groceries, or comparing insurance providers to get the best rates. Seek cost-saving opportunities without compromising your basic needs.

7. Emergency Fund: As part of your essential expenses, prioritize building an emergency fund. Set aside a portion of your income each month to establish a financial safety net for unexpected expenses or emergencies.

Remember, the allocation of income to essential expenses is just one component of your overall budget. Once your essential expenses are covered, you can allocate funds to other categories such as savings, debt repayment, and discretionary spending. By prioritizing and effectively allocating your income to essential expenses, you ensure that your basic needs are met and build a strong foundation for your financial well-being.

Determining Discretionary Spending

Determining discretionary spending involves identifying and allocating funds to non-essential expenses, such as entertainment, leisure activities, hobbies, and luxury items. Here's a guide on how to determine and manage your discretionary spending effectively:

1. Review Your Financial Priorities: Start by clarifying your financial priorities. Consider your long-term goals, such as saving for a down payment on a house, funding retirement, or paying off debt. Understanding your priorities will help you make informed decisions about how much to allocate to discretionary spending.

2. Calculate Available Discretionary Income: Calculate your available discretionary income by subtracting your essential expenses (such as housing, utilities, transportation, and debt payments) from your total income. The remaining amount represents the funds you can allocate towards discretionary spending.

3. Set a Discretionary Spending Limit: Establish a limit for your discretionary spending based on your financial goals and available discretionary income. This limit serves as a guideline to ensure that your non-essential expenses don't exceed a reasonable portion of your overall budget.

4. Prioritize Your Discretionary Spending: Prioritize your discretionary spending based on what brings you the most joy and aligns with your values. Allocate more funds to activities or purchases that hold greater significance to you, while being mindful of not overspending.

5. Allocate Funds to Different Categories: Divide your discretionary spending limit into categories based on your preferences and interests. Some common categories include entertainment (movies, concerts, subscriptions), dining out, hobbies, vacations, personal care, and shopping. Allocate a specific amount to each category to help you stay within your discretionary spending limit.

6. Track and Monitor Your Spending: Keep track of your discretionary expenses to ensure that you stay within your allocated limits. Use budgeting apps, spreadsheets, or financial management tools to track and categorize your expenses accurately. Regularly review your spending to identify any areas where you may need to make adjustments.

7. Make Conscious Spending Choices: Practice mindful spending by making conscious choices about your discretionary expenses. Consider the value and enjoyment you derive from each purchase or activity before committing your funds. Ask yourself if the expense aligns with your priorities and if there are more cost-effective alternatives available.

8. Look for Cost-Saving Opportunities: Explore ways to reduce costs within your discretionary spending categories. Look for discounts, promotions, or alternative options that allow you to enjoy similar experiences or items at a lower cost. Comparison shopping, using coupons, and taking advantage of loyalty programs are some strategies to consider.

9. Regularly Evaluate and Adjust: Periodically evaluate your discretionary spending habits and adjust your allocations as needed. Your financial priorities or circumstances may change, requiring you to reallocate funds or reprioritize your spending. Continuously review and refine your discretionary spending to align with your evolving goals and preferences.

By determining and managing your discretionary spending effectively, you can strike a balance between enjoying life's pleasures and working towards your long-term financial goals. Being mindful, setting limits, and making intentional choices will help you make the most of your discretionary funds while maintaining financial stability.

Saving For Emergencies And Future Needs

Saving money for emergencies and future needs is a crucial aspect of financial planning. It provides you with a safety net for unexpected expenses and allows you to work towards your long-term goals. Here's a guide on how to save money effectively for emergencies and future needs:

1. Set Financial Goals: Define your financial goals, including both short-term and long-term objectives. Short-term goals may include building an emergency fund, while long-term goals can involve saving for a down payment on a house, funding education, or planning for retirement. Having specific goals helps you stay focused and motivated.

2. Calculate Your Monthly Savings Capacity: Assess your income and expenses to determine how much you can save each month. Create a budget that allows you to cover your essential expenses while allocating a portion of your income towards savings.

3. Establish an Emergency Fund: Start by building an emergency fund, which serves as a financial cushion for unexpected expenses or income disruptions. Aim to save three to six months' worth of living expenses in your emergency fund. Gradually contribute to it until you reach this target.

4. Automate Your Savings: Set up automatic transfers from your checking account to your savings account. This way, a portion of your income is automatically saved each month, making it easier to stick to your savings goals.

5. Reduce Expenses and Increase Income: Look for opportunities to reduce your expenses and increase your income to free up more funds for savings. Cut back on discretionary spending, negotiate bills or contracts for better rates, or explore additional income streams such as freelancing or part-time work.

6. Prioritize Saving in Your Budget: Treat savings as a priority expense in your budget, just like any other essential expense. Allocate

a specific amount or percentage of your income towards savings before considering other discretionary expenses.

7. Track Your Progress: Regularly track and monitor your savings progress. Review your savings account statements, track your contributions, and celebrate milestones along the way. This helps you stay motivated and reassures you that you are moving closer to your financial goals.

8. Separate Savings for Different Goals: Consider creating separate savings accounts for different goals, such as emergency fund, retirement, or specific future needs. This allows you to track and allocate funds more effectively, ensuring that you don't dip into savings intended for a specific purpose.

9. Avoid Impulsive Spending: Practice mindful spending by thinking twice before making non-essential purchases. Differentiate between wants and needs, and consider the impact on your savings goals before making a purchase. Delay gratification when necessary and prioritize your long-term financial security.

10. Review and Adjust Regularly: Periodically review your savings plan and make adjustments as needed. Revisit your financial goals, reassess your savings capacity, and adjust your savings contributions accordingly. Changes in your income, expenses, or goals may require you to revise your savings strategy.

Remember, saving money is a habit that takes time and discipline to develop. Stay committed to your savings goals, be patient, and be prepared to make adjustments along the way. By consistently saving for emergencies and future needs, you can build a solid financial foundation and work towards a more secure and fulfilling financial future.

Chapter 4: Budgeting Techniques

The Envelope System

The envelope system is a budgeting technique that involves using physical envelopes to allocate and track your spending in different categories. Here's how the envelope system works:

1. Determine Your Budget Categories: Start by identifying the different categories in your budget, such as groceries, dining out, entertainment, transportation, clothing, and so on. These categories should align with your financial goals and spending priorities.

2. Assign Envelopes to Each Category: Label separate envelopes with the name of each budget category. You can use actual envelopes or create digital envelopes within a budgeting app or spreadsheet.

3. Allocate Cash to Envelopes: Decide how much money you want to allocate to each category for a specific period, such as a week or a month. Take out the corresponding amount of cash and place it in the respective envelopes. For digital envelopes, enter the allocated amounts.

4. Use Envelopes for Spending: Whenever you make a purchase in a particular category, use the money from the corresponding envelope. For example, if you are buying groceries, take the required cash from the "Groceries" envelope. If you're using digital envelopes, deduct the spent amount from the allocated total for that category.

5. Track Your Spending: Regularly track your expenses and update the amounts remaining in each envelope. This helps you stay aware of your spending in each category and ensures that you don't exceed your allocated amounts.

6. Adjust and Reallocate Funds: If you run out of money in one envelope before the designated time period is over, you have two options. You can either reallocate funds from other envelopes (if allowed) or temporarily halt spending in that category until you can replenish the envelope.

7. Replenish Envelopes Regularly: Replenish the envelopes at designated intervals, such as weekly or monthly, by allocating new funds.

This allows you to continue budgeting and spending within your planned limits.

Benefits of the Envelope System:

- Visual and Tangible: The envelope system provides a tangible representation of your budget, making it easier to understand and manage your spending.

- Limits Overspending: By using cash and having finite amounts in each envelope, you are more likely to think twice before making purchases and avoid overspending.

- Encourages Accountability: The envelope system promotes accountability as you physically see and manage the money you have allocated for each category.

- Simplifies Budgeting: This budgeting method is straightforward and easy to implement, especially for individuals who prefer a more hands-on approach to budgeting.

Considerations:

- Security: Carrying cash in envelopes can be a security concern. Ensure you keep your envelopes safe and consider alternatives like digital envelopes or using prepaid debit cards for added security.

- Flexibility: The envelope system may require some flexibility in case unexpected expenses arise. You may need to adjust your allocations or temporarily shift funds between envelopes.

- Record-Keeping: If using physical envelopes, it's essential to keep track of your spending manually. For digital envelopes, ensure you update your records promptly.

The envelope system can be a helpful

budgeting technique for those who prefer a more tangible and visual approach to managing their finances. It promotes awareness of spending habits, encourages disciplined spending, and helps you stay on track with your budget.

The 50/30/20 Rule

The 50/30/20 rule is a budgeting technique that suggests dividing your after-tax income into three categories: needs, wants, and savings. Here's how the 50/30/20 rule works:

1. Determine Your After-Tax Income: Calculate your income after taxes and any other deductions. This is the amount you'll use to allocate into the three categories.

2. Allocate 50% to Needs: Allocate 50% of your after-tax income to cover your essential needs. These include expenses such as rent or mortgage payments, utilities, groceries, transportation costs, insurance, minimum debt payments, and other essential bills.

3. Allocate 30% to Wants: Assign 30% of your after-tax income to your discretionary wants or non-essential expenses. These are expenses that enhance your lifestyle but are not necessary for your basic needs. Examples include dining out, entertainment, travel, hobbies, and other non-essential purchases.

4. Allocate 20% to Savings: Allocate 20% of your after-tax income to savings and debt repayment. This category includes building an emergency fund, saving for retirement, paying off debts beyond the minimum payments, and investing for future goals.

5. Adjust and Track Your Spending: Monitor your spending within each category to ensure you're staying within the allocated percentages. Adjust your expenses as needed to align with the 50/30/20 rule. Regularly review your budget and make adjustments based on changes in your income or financial goals.

Benefits of the 50/30/20 Rule:

- Simplicity: The 50/30/20 rule provides a straightforward framework for budgeting, making it easy to understand and implement.

- Balance: It helps achieve a balance between meeting your essential needs, enjoying discretionary spending, and saving for the future.

- Flexibility: The rule allows for some flexibility within the 30% wants category, giving you discretion over how you allocate your non-essential spending.

- Savings Focus: By allocating 20% of your income to savings, the 50/30/20 rule emphasizes the importance of building an emergency fund and saving for future financial goals.

Considerations:

- Personal Circumstances: The 50/30/20 rule may not be suitable for everyone, as individual financial situations and priorities can vary. Adjustments may be necessary based on your specific needs and goals.

- High Expenses or Debt: If your essential expenses or debt payments exceed 50% of your income, you may need to make adjustments to ensure you can cover your needs adequately.

- Savings Goals: Depending on your financial goals, you might need to allocate more than 20% to savings to accelerate debt repayment or save for specific milestones.

- Geographic Differences: Keep in mind that the 50/30/20 rule is a general guideline and may need to be adjusted based on your location and cost of living.

The 50/30/20 rule can be a useful starting point for creating a balanced budget and prioritizing your spending and savings. However, it's essential to evaluate your own financial situation and make adjustments to ensure your budget aligns with your specific needs, goals, and lifestyle.

Zero-Based Budgeting

Zero-based budgeting (ZBB) is a budgeting technique that requires you to allocate your income to various expenses and savings categories from scratch, starting with a zero balance for each category. Here's how zero-based budgeting works:

1. Determine Your Income: Begin by identifying your total income for a specific period, such as a month. This includes all sources of income, such as salaries, wages, freelance earnings, and any other inflows.

2. Identify Your Expenses: Make a comprehensive list of all your expenses. Categorize them into fixed expenses (such as rent/mortgage, utilities, insurance), variable expenses (such as groceries, transportation, entertainment), and discretionary expenses (such as dining out, hobbies, shopping).

3. Assign Every Dollar a Job: With zero-based budgeting, your goal is to allocate every dollar of your income to an expense or savings category. Start by assigning your income to cover your fixed expenses first, ensuring that these essential costs are fully funded.

4. Prioritize and Allocate Funds: Once your fixed expenses are covered, prioritize your remaining income to allocate it to your variable and discretionary expenses based on their importance and relevance to your financial goals. Consider factors such as your needs, values, and long-term objectives.

5. Create a Budget Worksheet: Use a budgeting tool, spreadsheet, or budgeting app to create a worksheet that outlines your income and expenses. Allocate the appropriate amounts to each category, subtracting the allocated amounts from your income until you reach a zero balance.

6. Review and Adjust: Regularly review your budget to ensure that it aligns with your financial goals and that you are not overspending in any category. Adjust your allocations as necessary, particularly if your income or expenses change over time.

Benefits of Zero-Based Budgeting:

- Increased Awareness: Zero-based budgeting requires you to evaluate every expense and make intentional decisions about how to allocate your income. This promotes a deeper understanding of your financial situation and spending habits.

- Efficient Resource Allocation: By starting from zero and scrutinizing every expense, zero-based budgeting encourages you to prioritize your resources and allocate them to the areas that provide the most value and align with your goals.

- Cost Control: Zero-based budgeting helps identify areas where you may be overspending and prompts you to make adjustments. It can lead to more effective cost control and the elimination of unnecessary expenses.

- Flexibility and Adaptability: Zero-based budgeting allows you to adapt your budget more easily to changes in your income or financial priorities. It provides the flexibility to reallocate funds based on evolving circumstances.

Considerations:

- Time and Effort: Zero-based budgeting requires more time and effort compared to other budgeting methods because you are starting from scratch each time. It involves evaluating and allocating every expense, which can be time-consuming.

- Initial Learning Curve: If you're new to budgeting or have not used zero-based budgeting before, there may be a learning curve to understand the process and effectively allocate your income.

- Varied Income Months: Zero-based budgeting can be more challenging if your income fluctuates significantly from month to month. In such cases, you may need to adjust your allocations accordingly.

Zero-based budgeting can be a powerful tool for gaining control over your finances, ensuring that your money is allocated according to your priorities, and eliminating unnecessary expenses. It encourages a proactive approach to budgeting and empowers you to make informed decisions about your financial resources.

Automated Budgeting Tools

Automated budgeting tools are software applications or online platforms that help individuals and households manage their finances by automating various aspects of budgeting and expense tracking. These tools offer features that simplify the budgeting process and provide insights into spending habits. Here are some benefits and popular examples of automated budgeting tools:

Benefits of Automated Budgeting Tools:

1. Expense Tracking: Automated budgeting tools automatically track your income and expenses by linking to your bank accounts, credit cards, and other financial accounts. This eliminates the need for manual entry and ensures accurate and up-to-date records of your transactions.

2. Categorization and Analysis: These tools categorize your expenses into different categories (e.g., groceries, transportation, entertainment) to provide a clear overview of your spending patterns. They often generate visual reports and charts, allowing you to analyze your spending habits and identify areas for improvement.

3. Budget Creation and Management: Automated budgeting tools facilitate the creation and management of budgets. They help you set financial goals, allocate funds to different categories, and track your progress. Some tools provide customizable budget templates or recommendations based on your income and spending patterns.

4. Bill Reminders and Alerts: Many budgeting tools offer bill reminder features to help you stay on top of your financial obligations. They can send notifications or alerts when bills are due, helping you avoid late payments and associated fees.

5. Goal Tracking: Automated budgeting tools often include goal tracking features that allow you to set and monitor your progress toward financial goals such as saving for a vacation, paying off debt, or building an emergency fund. They provide visual representations of your progress to keep you motivated.

6. Synchronization Across Devices: Most automated budgeting tools are accessible through mobile apps and web interfaces, ensuring synchronization across multiple devices. This allows you to manage your budget and track expenses on-the-go, from anywhere.

Popular Automated Budgeting Tools:

1. Mint: Mint is a free budgeting tool that helps you track expenses, set financial goals, and create budgets. It syncs with your financial accounts, categorizes transactions, and provides insights into your spending habits.

2. You Need a Budget (YNAB): YNAB is a paid budgeting tool known for its envelope budgeting system. It helps you allocate funds, tracks your spending, and offers educational resources to help you improve your financial management skills.

3. Personal Capital: Personal Capital is a comprehensive financial management tool that combines budgeting, investment tracking, and retirement planning. It provides a holistic view of your finances and allows you to track your net worth.

4. PocketGuard: PocketGuard is a free app that focuses on helping you manage your day-to-day spending. It categorizes transactions, provides budgeting recommendations, and helps you stay within your spending limits.

5. Goodbudget: Goodbudget is a digital envelope budgeting tool that simulates the traditional envelope system. It allows you to allocate funds to different envelopes (categories) and tracks your spending accordingly.

6. Tiller Money: Tiller Money is a spreadsheet-based budgeting tool that automates data importing from your financial accounts into customizable Google Sheets or Microsoft Excel templates. It provides flexibility and control over your budgeting process.

When choosing an automated budgeting tool, consider factors such as ease of use, features that align with your needs, security measures, customer support, and any associated costs. Each tool has its own unique features, so it's essential to find one that suits your preferences and helps you effectively manage your finances.

Chapter 5: Managing Debt

Understanding Different Types of Debt

Understanding different types of debt is essential for managing your finances effectively. Here are some common types of debt:

1. Credit Card Debt: This type of debt arises when you use a credit card to make purchases or cash advances. If you don't pay off the full balance by the due date, interest charges apply, and the debt can accumulate over time. Credit card debt often carries high-interest rates, making it important to manage and pay it off promptly.

2. Student Loans: Student loans are taken out to finance education expenses. They can be issued by the government or private lenders. Student loans typically have specific repayment terms, including interest rates and grace periods. It's crucial to understand the terms and create a plan for repayment.

3. Mortgage Loans: A mortgage is a loan used to finance the purchase of a home. It is a long-term debt with regular monthly payments over a set period. The terms of a mortgage loan include interest rates, loan duration, and collateral (the property itself).

4. Auto Loans: Auto loans are taken to finance the purchase of a vehicle. Like mortgages, they have specific terms, including interest rates and repayment periods. Failure to make timely payments can result in repossession of the vehicle.

5. Personal Loans: Personal loans are unsecured loans that can be used for various purposes, such as debt consolidation, home improvements, or unexpected expenses. Personal loans typically have fixed interest rates and repayment terms.

6. Payday Loans: Payday loans are short-term, high-interest loans that are usually due on the borrower's next payday. They are typically small-dollar amounts and are intended to be a temporary solution for immediate cash needs. However, payday loans often come with extremely high-interest rates and fees, making them a costly form of borrowing.

7. Medical Debt: Medical debt arises when you have unpaid medical bills for healthcare services or treatments. It can result from out-of-pocket expenses not covered by insurance or from being uninsured. Medical debt may have varying repayment options and interest rates depending on the healthcare provider or collection agency.

8. Business Loans: Business loans are borrowed by entrepreneurs to start or expand their businesses. These loans may have different terms and interest rates, depending on the purpose, size, and creditworthiness of the business.

9. Overdrafts and Lines of Credit: Overdrafts occur when you spend more money than you have available in your bank account, resulting in a negative balance. Overdrafts are typically subject to fees and high-interest rates. Lines of credit, on the other hand, provide access to a predetermined credit limit that can be used as needed, similar to a credit card.

It's important to note that not all debt is inherently negative. Some forms of debt, such as a mortgage or business loan, can be strategic and beneficial when managed responsibly and used to generate assets or invest in future growth.

Understanding the different types of debt can help you make informed decisions about borrowing, prioritize debt repayment, and effectively manage your overall financial health. It's crucial to consider interest rates, repayment terms, and your ability to comfortably meet payment obligations when taking on any form of debt.

Prioritizing Debt Repayment

Prioritizing debt repayment is crucial for improving your financial situation and becoming debt-free. Here are some steps to help you prioritize your debt repayment:

1. Assess Your Debt: Begin by making a list of all your debts, including the outstanding balance, interest rate, minimum monthly payment, and due dates. This will give you a clear picture of your overall debt burden.

2. Identify High-Interest Debts: Sort your debts by interest rate, with the highest interest rate at the top. High-interest debts cost you more over time, so it's generally advisable to prioritize paying them off first.

3. Consider Debt Snowball or Debt Avalanche Method: There are two popular strategies for prioritizing debt repayment: the debt snowball method and the debt avalanche method.

- Debt Snowball Method: With the debt snowball method, you focus on paying off the smallest debts first, regardless of interest rates. Start by making extra payments on the smallest debt while making minimum payments on the others. Once the smallest debt is paid off, roll the amount you were paying towards that debt into the next smallest debt. Repeat this process until all debts are paid off.

- Debt Avalanche Method: The debt avalanche method involves prioritizing debts based on their interest rates. Start by making extra payments on the debt with the highest interest rate while making minimum payments on the others. Once the highest interest debt is paid off, move to the one with the next highest interest rate. Continue this process until all debts are cleared.

Choose the method that aligns best with your preferences and financial situation. The debt snowball method may provide psychological motivation as you see debts being paid off sooner, while the debt avalanche method may save you more money on interest in the long run.

4. Maintain Minimum Payments: While focusing on your prioritized debt, make sure to continue making at least the minimum monthly payments on all your other debts. This ensures that you avoid late fees, penalties, and negative impacts on your credit score.

5. Explore Debt Consolidation or Refinancing: Consider options to consolidate your debts into a single loan or refinance existing debts to potentially secure a lower interest rate. This can simplify your repayment process and potentially save you money on interest.

6. Increase Your Debt Repayment Efforts: Look for ways to free up additional money to put towards debt repayment. This can include cutting back on discretionary expenses, finding ways to increase your income, or reallocating funds from non-essential areas of your budget.

7. Stay Committed and Track Progress: Consistency is key to debt repayment. Stay committed to your debt repayment plan and track your progress regularly. Celebrate milestones along the way to maintain motivation.

Remember, prioritizing debt repayment requires discipline and patience. It's important to balance debt repayment with maintaining a basic level of financial security and meeting your essential living expenses.

If you're facing challenges or feeling overwhelmed, consider seeking advice from a financial advisor or credit counselling service. They can provide personalized guidance based on your specific financial situation and help you develop a repayment plan tailored to your needs.

Strategies For Reducing Debt

Reducing debt requires a combination of discipline, careful planning, and strategic approaches. Here are several effective strategies for reducing debt:

1. Create a Budget: Develop a comprehensive budget that tracks your income and expenses. This will help you identify areas where you can cut back on spending and allocate more funds towards debt repayment.

2. Cut Expenses: Review your expenses and look for ways to reduce discretionary spending. Consider making lifestyle adjustments such as dining out less frequently, canceling unnecessary subscriptions, or finding cost-effective alternatives for entertainment and leisure activities.

3. Increase Income: Explore opportunities to increase your income. This could involve taking on a side job, freelancing, monetizing a hobby, or seeking a higher-paying job. The additional income can be directly allocated towards debt repayment.

4. Snowball or Avalanche Method: Choose a debt repayment strategy that suits you best - the debt snowball or the debt avalanche method (explained in the previous response). Stick to your chosen method and consistently make extra payments towards your debts.

5. Negotiate Lower Interest Rates: Contact your creditors and explore the possibility of negotiating lower interest rates on your debts. This can help reduce the overall amount you need to pay and accelerate your debt repayment progress.

6. Debt Consolidation: Consider consolidating your debts into a single loan with a lower interest rate. Debt consolidation can simplify your repayment process and potentially save you money on interest. However, carefully evaluate the terms and fees associated with consolidation before making a decision.

7. Use Windfalls and Bonuses Wisely: If you receive unexpected windfalls such as tax refunds, bonuses, or monetary gifts, resist the

temptation to splurge and instead allocate them towards debt repayment. These additional funds can make a significant impact on reducing your debt burden.

8. Seek Professional Help: If your debt situation feels overwhelming or you're having difficulty managing it on your own, consider consulting a financial advisor or credit counselling service. They can provide personalized guidance, negotiate with creditors on your behalf, and help you develop a tailored debt repayment plan.

9. Avoid Taking on New Debt: While focusing on debt reduction, be mindful of your spending habits and avoid taking on new debt. Resist the urge to use credit cards for unnecessary purchases or taking out additional loans unless absolutely necessary.

10. Stay Motivated and Celebrate Milestones: Reducing debt takes time and effort, so it's important to stay motivated along the way. Celebrate small milestones, such as paying off a particular debt or reaching a certain percentage of overall debt reduction. Recognizing progress can help you maintain momentum and continue on your debt reduction journey.

Remember, reducing debt is a gradual process. Be patient, stay committed to your plan, and regularly reassess and adjust your strategies as needed. With persistence and smart financial management, you can work towards becoming debt-free and achieving financial freedom.

Chapter 6: Tracking and Adjusting Your Budget

The Importance of Tracking Expenses

Tracking expenses is crucial for effective financial management. Here are some key reasons why tracking expenses is important:

1. Awareness and Understanding: Tracking your expenses allows you to have a clear understanding of where your money is going. It provides insight into your spending habits, patterns, and areas where you may be overspending. This awareness is the first step towards making informed financial decisions.

2. Budgeting: Expense tracking is essential for creating and maintaining a budget. By knowing your income and tracking your expenses, you can allocate your money wisely, set financial goals, and ensure that you're not spending more than you earn. Tracking expenses helps you stay accountable to your budget and make adjustments as needed.

3. Identifying Saving Opportunities: When you track your expenses, you can identify areas where you can potentially cut costs and save money. It allows you to spot unnecessary or excessive expenses that can be eliminated or reduced. Small adjustments in spending habits, such as reducing dining out or entertainment expenses, can add up to significant savings over time.

4. Debt Management: Tracking expenses helps you manage your debts effectively. By understanding your spending patterns, you can allocate more funds towards debt repayment, avoid accumulating additional debt, and make timely payments to avoid late fees or penalties.

5. Financial Goal Setting: When you track your expenses, you gain a better understanding of your financial capabilities and limitations. This knowledge allows you to set realistic financial goals, such as saving for emergencies, retirement, a down payment on a home, or a vacation. Tracking expenses helps you prioritize your goals and make progress towards achieving them.

6. Decision Making: When you have accurate and up-to-date information about your expenses, you can make informed decisions about major purchases, investments, and financial commitments. Tracking expenses gives you a clear picture of your financial situation, allowing you to evaluate the feasibility and impact of various financial choices.

7. Tax Preparation: Tracking your expenses makes tax preparation much easier. By maintaining organized records of your expenses, you can ensure that you claim all eligible deductions and credits, maximize your tax savings, and avoid potential errors or omissions.

8. Financial Awareness and Control: Tracking expenses empowers you to take control of your finances. It helps you develop a sense of financial discipline, as you become more mindful of your spending choices and their impact on your overall financial well-being. By actively monitoring your expenses, you can make conscious decisions aligned with your financial goals.

There are various methods and tools available to track expenses, including budgeting apps, spreadsheets, or even simple pen and paper. Choose a method that suits your preferences and lifestyle, and make it a habit to regularly review and analyze your expenses. The ongoing practice of tracking expenses will provide valuable insights and help you make better financial decisions.

Making Adjustments As Needed

Making adjustments to your expense tracking process is essential to ensure its effectiveness and relevance over time. Here are some considerations for making adjustments:

1. Review Your Tracking Method: Assess the method you are using to track expenses and determine if it is still suitable for your needs. If you find it cumbersome or time-consuming, consider exploring alternative methods or digital tools that may streamline the process.

2. Simplify Categories: If you find that your expense categories are too detailed or overwhelming, consider simplifying them. Having fewer categories can make it easier to track and analyze your spending patterns. However, ensure that the simplified categories still capture the necessary information for effective budgeting and financial analysis.

3. Fine-tune Budget Estimates: Periodically review your budget estimates to ensure they align with your current financial situation. If you consistently overspend in certain categories or find that some estimates are too restrictive, make adjustments accordingly. This allows for a more realistic and achievable budget.

4. Revisit Priorities: As your financial goals and priorities evolve, it may be necessary to adjust the allocation of your resources. Consider whether any changes are needed in your budget to reflect new goals or changes in circumstances. This may involve reallocating funds from one category to another or identifying areas where you can cut back to free up money for higher-priority expenses.

5. Track Irregular or Seasonal Expenses: Take into account irregular or seasonal expenses that may not occur every month but can significantly impact your budget. Examples include holiday spending, annual insurance premiums, or car maintenance. Anticipate these expenses and allocate funds accordingly so that you are prepared when they arise.

6. Embrace Technology: Explore the use of budgeting apps or personal finance software that can automate expense tracking and provide real-time insights into your spending habits. These tools can help streamline the process, provide visualizations, and generate reports to facilitate analysis and decision-making.

7. Regularly Evaluate Progress: Periodically review your expense tracking data to assess your progress towards financial goals and identify areas for improvement. Look for trends or patterns in your spending that may require attention or adjustments. This evaluation allows you to make informed decisions and stay on track with your financial objectives.

8. Seek Input and Support: Discuss your budget and expense tracking process with a trusted friend, family member, or financial advisor. They can provide fresh perspectives, offer suggestions for improvement, and hold you accountable to your financial goals.

Remember, tracking expenses is not a static process. It should adapt to your changing circumstances, financial goals, and personal preferences. By regularly assessing and making adjustments as needed, you can maintain an effective expense tracking system that supports your financial well-being and helps you achieve your desired financial outcomes.

Tips For Staying On Track

Staying on track with tracking expenses can be challenging, but it's crucial for effective financial management. Here are some tips to help you stay committed and consistent with your expense tracking:

1. Set Clear Goals: Define your financial goals and connect them to your expense tracking efforts. Whether it's paying off debt, saving for a down payment, or building an emergency fund, having a clear purpose will motivate you to stay on track.

2. Make it a Routine: Incorporate expense tracking into your daily or weekly routine. Set aside dedicated time to update your expense records, review your spending, and reconcile your budget. Consistency is key, so find a schedule that works for you and stick to it.

3. Choose a Method That Works for You: Find an expense tracking method that suits your preferences and lifestyle. Whether it's using a budgeting app, a spreadsheet, or a dedicated notebook, select a method that you find intuitive and easy to use. The more seamless the process, the more likely you are to stick with it.

4. Automate Whenever Possible: Take advantage of technology and automation to simplify expense tracking. Use apps or software that can automatically sync your transactions from bank accounts and credit cards, reducing the manual data entry required. This can save time and ensure accuracy in your records.

5. Keep Receipts and Documentation: Make it a habit to keep receipts for your purchases and other relevant documentation, such as bills or invoices. This will help you accurately track and categorize expenses. Consider using digital tools to capture and store receipts electronically for easy access and organization.

6. Set Reminders and Alerts: Use reminders or alerts on your phone or through your expense tracking app to prompt you to update your expenses regularly. These reminders can serve as a helpful nudge to stay on top of your tracking routine.

7. Track All Expenses: Be diligent about tracking all your expenses, no matter how small. Even minor expenses can add up over time, so capturing every transaction gives you a comprehensive view of your spending habits. Consider using a mobile app that allows you to track expenses on the go, making it easier to record expenses in real-time.

8. Stay Accountable: Share your expense tracking goals with a trusted friend, family member, or an accountability partner. Discuss your progress regularly and hold each other accountable for staying on track. Celebrate milestones together and provide support when facing challenges.

9. Review and Analyze: Regularly review and analyze your expense tracking data. Look for patterns, trends, and areas where you can make improvements. Use the insights gained from your analysis to make informed decisions about your spending and budget adjustments.

10. Stay Motivated: Find ways to stay motivated and engaged with your expense tracking process. This could include visualizing your financial goals, rewarding yourself for milestones achieved, or seeking inspiration from personal finance resources or success stories.

Remember that tracking expenses is an ongoing process that requires persistence and discipline. Stay committed, be patient with yourself, and view expense tracking as a valuable tool for improving your financial well-being. Over time, you will develop better financial habits and gain greater control over your money.

Chapter 7: Saving and Investing

The Importance of Saving

Saving money is of paramount importance for several reasons:

1. Emergency Fund: Having savings allows you to build an emergency fund, which serves as a financial safety net. Life is unpredictable, and unexpected expenses such as medical emergencies, car repairs, or job loss can arise. An emergency fund provides you with a cushion to handle these situations without resorting to high-interest debt or financial stress.

2. Financial Stability: Saving money provides financial stability and peace of mind. It allows you to cover your daily living expenses, pay bills on time, and avoid living pay-check to pay-check. Having savings provides a sense of security, reduces anxiety about financial uncertainties, and helps you withstand unexpected financial shocks.

3. Achieving Financial Goals: Saving is essential for reaching long-term financial goals. Whether it's buying a home, funding education, starting a business, or retiring comfortably, having savings helps you accumulate the necessary funds over time. Regular contributions to savings accounts or investment vehicles enable you to make progress towards these goals.

4. Retirement Planning: Saving for retirement is crucial to ensure financial security in your later years. The earlier you start saving for retirement, the more time your savings have to grow through compound interest and investment returns. Building a retirement nest egg allows you to maintain your lifestyle and cover expenses when you're no longer working.

5. Financial Independence: Saving money empowers you to achieve financial independence. It provides you with the freedom to make choices based on your preferences rather than being driven solely by financial constraints. Saving gives you the flexibility to pursue opportunities, change careers, take time off work, or pursue your passions without being reliant on each pay-check.

6. Avoiding Debt and Interest Payments: Saving helps you avoid unnecessary debt and interest payments. By having savings to cover expenses, you can avoid relying on credit cards or loans for everyday needs. This reduces the risk of falling into a cycle of debt and saves you money by avoiding high-interest charges.

7. Taking Advantage of Opportunities: Having savings allows you to seize opportunities when they arise. Whether it's an investment opportunity, a chance to travel, or a major purchase at a discounted price, having funds readily available enables you to take advantage of favourable situations and make the most of them.

8. Legacy Planning: Saving money allows you to leave a financial legacy for your loved ones. By accumulating wealth, you can pass on assets, provide for your family's future, or support causes that are important to you. Saving enables you to create a lasting impact and support future generations.

Saving money requires discipline, prioritization, and a commitment to consistently allocate a portion of your income towards savings. Even small savings contributions can add up over time and make a significant difference in your financial well-being. Start saving early, set realistic goals, and make saving a habit to secure your financial future.

Differentiating Between Short-Term and Long-Term Goals

Differentiating between short-term and long-term financial goals is important for effective financial planning. Here's how you can distinguish between the two:

Short-Term Financial Goals:

1. Timeframe: Short-term goals typically have a timeframe of less than one year or are goals that you want to achieve in the near future.

2. Immediate Needs and Wants: Short-term goals usually focus on meeting immediate needs and wants, such as paying off small debts, saving for a vacation, or purchasing a new appliance.

3. Tangible and Specific: Short-term goals are often more concrete and specific. They are typically measurable and have a clear target amount or objective.

4. Regular Monitoring and Quick Results: Short-term goals require frequent monitoring and can be achieved relatively quickly. They often involve regular contributions or actions to reach the desired outcome within a short timeframe.

Examples of short-term financial goals include:

- Building an emergency fund to cover three months' worth of living expenses.
- Paying off credit card debt within the next six months.
- Saving for a down payment on a car within a year.
- Taking a vacation within the next few months.
- Purchasing new furniture or electronics in the near future.

Long-Term Financial Goals:

1. Timeframe: Long-term goals are typically those that you aim to achieve in the distant future, usually beyond one year.

2. Future Planning: Long-term goals are focused on major life events, financial security, and planning for the future, such as retirement planning, buying a home, or funding a child's education.

3. Strategic and Flexible: Long-term goals require strategic planning and flexibility as circumstances may change over time. They often involve multiple steps and a longer time horizon to achieve.

4. Regular Review and Adjustments: Long-term goals need regular review and adjustments to stay on track. They require consistent saving, investing, and monitoring progress towards the desired outcome.

Examples of long-term financial goals include:

- Saving for retirement to maintain a comfortable lifestyle after you stop working.
- Paying off a mortgage and owning a home outright.
- Building a college fund for your child's education.
- Starting a business or pursuing self-employment in the future.
- Achieving financial independence and early retirement.

It's important to note that short-term and long-term financial goals are interconnected. Achieving short-term goals can contribute to progress towards long-term goals. By prioritizing and balancing your financial resources between short-term and long-term goals, you can create a comprehensive financial plan that addresses your immediate needs while building a secure financial future.

Introduction to Basic Investment Options

1. Stocks: Stocks represent ownership shares in publicly traded companies. When you buy stocks, you become a shareholder and have the potential to earn returns through capital appreciation (the stock price increasing) and dividends (payments made by the company to shareholders). Investing in individual stocks requires research and knowledge about the company's fundamentals, market conditions, and risk tolerance.

2. Bonds: Bonds are debt securities issued by governments, municipalities, and corporations. When you buy a bond, you are essentially lending money to the issuer in exchange for regular interest payments and the return of the principal amount at maturity. Bonds are generally considered lower risk compared to stocks, but they offer lower potential returns.

3. Mutual Funds: Mutual funds pool money from multiple investors to invest in a diversified portfolio of stocks, bonds, or other assets. They are managed by professional fund managers who make investment decisions on behalf of the investors. Mutual funds provide diversification, convenience, and access to professional management. They can be categorized based on different investment objectives and asset classes.

4. Exchange-Traded Funds (ETFs): ETFs are similar to mutual funds but trade on stock exchanges like individual stocks. They represent a basket of securities that can include stocks, bonds, commodities, or other assets. ETFs offer diversification, flexibility, and the ability to trade throughout the day. They can track various market indices or follow specific investment strategies.

5. Real Estate Investment Trusts (REITs): REITs are investment vehicles that own and operate income-generating real estate properties. They allow investors to participate in real estate ownership without directly owning and managing properties. REITs provide the potential

for income through rental payments and capital appreciation. They can focus on specific property types like residential, commercial, or industrial real estate.

6. Certificate of Deposit (CD): CDs are time deposits offered by banks with fixed maturity dates and predetermined interest rates. They provide a fixed rate of return over a specified period, usually ranging from a few months to several years. CDs are considered lower risk because they are insured by the FDIC in the United States (up to certain limits), but they offer relatively lower returns compared to other investment options.

7. Savings Accounts: Savings accounts are deposit accounts offered by banks that allow you to earn interest on your deposited funds. They provide a safe place to hold your cash, maintain liquidity, and earn some interest. However, the interest rates on savings accounts are typically lower compared to other investment options.

It's important to note that each investment option carries its own risks, potential returns, and suitability for different financial goals and risk tolerance levels. Before making any investment decisions, it's recommended to research and consider factors such as your financial objectives, time horizon, risk tolerance, and consult with a financial advisor or professional to ensure your investment choices align with your overall financial plan.

Chapter 8: Budgeting for Special Circumstances

Budgeting for Irregular Income

Budgeting for irregular income can be challenging but with careful planning and flexibility, it's possible to effectively manage your finances. Here are some tips for budgeting with irregular income:

1. Track and Average Your Income: Start by tracking your income over a longer period, such as six months or a year. Calculate the average income you receive during that period. This will give you a baseline for your budgeting.

2. Determine Fixed Expenses: Identify your fixed expenses, such as rent/mortgage payments, utilities, insurance premiums, and loan payments. These expenses remain relatively constant each month and should be prioritized in your budget.

3. Create a Bare-Bones Budget: Develop a budget based on your minimum essential expenses. This includes basic necessities like food, transportation, and healthcare. Allocate funds to cover these expenses even during low-income months.

4. Build an Emergency Fund: Set aside a portion of your income to build an emergency fund. This fund will provide a buffer during months when your income is lower than average or when unexpected expenses arise. Aim to save three to six months' worth of living expenses.

5. Prioritize Savings: Allocate a portion of your income towards savings, even if it's a small amount. Save for short-term goals like vacations or major purchases and long-term goals like retirement. Regular savings contributions will help smooth out income fluctuations and work towards financial stability.

6. Use a Variable Expense Category: Categorize discretionary expenses like entertainment, dining out, and hobbies as variable expenses. These are expenses that can be adjusted based on your income for a particular month. Allocate funds for variable expenses based on the income you expect to receive.

7. Flexibility and Adjustments: Embrace flexibility in your budgeting approach. During months of higher income, allocate the surplus towards savings or debt repayment. In months with lower income, cut back on variable expenses and non-essential spending.

8. Plan for Inconsistent Expenses: Consider irregular expenses that occur periodically but not monthly, such as annual subscriptions, vehicle maintenance, or holiday gifts. Set aside funds each month to anticipate these expenses when they arise.

9. Evaluate and Adjust Regularly: Review your budget regularly and make adjustments as needed. Track your actual income and expenses, compare them to your budget, and make necessary modifications to ensure you stay on track.

10. Maintain Financial Discipline: Stick to your budgeting plan and avoid impulsive spending. Stay disciplined and make conscious choices based on your financial goals and priorities.

Budgeting with irregular income requires careful planning, adaptability, and diligent tracking of your finances. By creating a realistic budget, building an emergency fund, and prioritizing savings, you can navigate the fluctuations of irregular income and maintain financial stability.

Budgeting for Major Life Events (e.g., Weddings , Home Buying)

Budgeting for major life events is essential to ensure that you have the necessary funds to cover significant expenses. Whether it's a wedding, buying a home, starting a family, or pursuing higher education, here are some steps to help you budget for these milestones:

1. Identify the Event and Set a Timeline: Clearly define the major life event and determine the timeframe in which you plan to achieve it. This will help you establish a realistic savings goal and create a timeline for your budgeting.

2. Research and Estimate Costs: Conduct thorough research to understand the costs associated with the event. Consider all the expenses involved, such as venue rental, catering, decorations, attire, travel, legal fees, education tuition, down payment for a home, or any other relevant expenses. Use this information to estimate the total amount you need to save.

3. Create a Separate Savings Account: Open a dedicated savings account specifically for the major life event. Having a separate account allows you to track your progress more effectively and prevents the funds from being mixed with your regular expenses.

4. Set a Savings Goal: Based on your research and estimated costs, establish a savings goal for the event. Break down the total amount into smaller monthly or quarterly savings targets to make it more manageable. Determine how much you need to save each month to reach your goal within the desired timeframe.

5. Adjust Your Budget: Review your current budget and make adjustments to allocate funds towards saving for the major life event. Identify areas where you can reduce discretionary spending or find ways to increase your income to save more. Cut back on non-essential expenses and redirect those funds to your savings account.

6. Automate Savings: Consider setting up automatic transfers from your regular bank account to the dedicated savings account for the event. This way, a portion of your income will be consistently saved without the need for manual transfers.

7. Prioritize Savings: Make saving for the major life event a financial priority. Treat it as a fixed expense and contribute to it before allocating funds to discretionary spending. Regularly monitor your progress towards your savings goal and adjust your budget as needed.

8. Explore Additional Funding Sources: If the savings target seems challenging to achieve within your desired timeframe, consider additional funding sources. This could include seeking financial assistance from family members, exploring low-interest loans or grants, or looking for opportunities to earn extra income through part-time work or side gigs.

9. Regularly Review and Adjust: Continuously monitor your budget and savings progress. Revisit your savings goal, timeline, and estimated costs periodically to ensure they are still accurate. Make adjustments to your budget and savings plan as circumstances change.

10. Seek Professional Advice if Needed: For complex events like buying a home or planning for retirement, consider consulting with a financial advisor who can provide guidance and help you make informed financial decisions.

By planning ahead, setting specific savings goals, and making adjustments to your budget, you can successfully budget for major life events. Remember to remain disciplined, stay focused on your savings goal, and make financial choices that align with your priorities.

Budgeting for students and young adults

Budgeting is crucial for students and young adults as it helps establish good financial habits and sets the foundation for a secure financial future. Here are some steps to help with budgeting:

1. Determine Income: Calculate your income from various sources such as part-time jobs, internships, scholarships, or financial aid. Consider any regular allowances or contributions from family members as well.

2. Track Expenses: Keep a record of all your expenses for a month or two to understand where your money is going. Categorize expenses into fixed (e.g., rent, utilities) and variable (e.g., dining out, entertainment) to identify areas where you can potentially reduce spending.

3. Create a Budget: Based on your income and expense tracking, create a budget that aligns with your financial goals. Allocate your income towards different categories such as rent, utilities, groceries, transportation, entertainment, savings, and debt repayment (if applicable).

4. Prioritize Essentials: Ensure that essential expenses like rent, utilities, and groceries are covered first. These should be your top priorities in your budget to maintain a stable living situation.

5. Limit Discretionary Spending: Be mindful of discretionary expenses like eating out, entertainment, and shopping. Set a reasonable limit for these categories and look for cost-effective alternatives or opportunities to save money.

6. Set Savings Goals: Establish savings goals to build an emergency fund or save for specific future needs like travel, further education, or purchasing a car. Aim to save a certain percentage of your income each month and automate your savings if possible.

7. Minimize Debt: If you have student loans or credit card debt, create a plan to manage and reduce it. Allocate a portion of your income towards debt repayment, paying more than the minimum payment

whenever possible. Consider options like consolidating loans or seeking assistance if you're struggling with repayment.

8. Seek Student Discounts: Take advantage of student discounts offered by various retailers, entertainment venues, and service providers. This can help you save money on essential items and activities.

9. Plan for Irregular Expenses: Anticipate irregular expenses like textbooks, school supplies, and healthcare costs. Set aside funds each month to prepare for these expenses when they arise.

10. Review and Adjust: Regularly review your budget to track your progress and make adjustments as needed. Reflect on your spending habits and financial goals to ensure your budget remains realistic and effective.

11. Seek Financial Education: Take advantage of resources available to enhance your financial knowledge. Attend workshops, read books, or explore online resources to gain a better understanding of personal finance and money management.

Remember, budgeting is an ongoing process, and it may take time to refine your budgeting skills. Stay committed to your financial goals, be mindful of your spending, and adapt your budget as your circumstances change.

Chapter 9: Overcoming Budgeting Challenges

Dealing With Unexpected Expenses

Dealing with unexpected expenses can be challenging, but with proper planning and financial resilience, you can navigate these situations more effectively. Here are some steps to help you handle unexpected expenses:

1. Emergency Fund: Having an emergency fund is crucial to handle unexpected expenses. Aim to save three to six months' worth of living expenses in a separate savings account. If you don't have an emergency fund, start building one as soon as possible by setting aside a portion of your income each month.

2. Assess the Situation: Evaluate the nature and urgency of the unexpected expense. Determine if it's a true emergency that requires immediate attention or if it can be managed over time. This assessment will help you prioritize and allocate your resources effectively.

3. Review Your Budget: Take a close look at your budget and identify areas where you can temporarily reduce or eliminate expenses to free up funds for the unexpected expense. Cut back on non-essential spending and redirect those funds to cover the urgent need.

4. Seek Alternatives: Explore alternative solutions to mitigate the financial impact of the unexpected expense. For example, if you're facing a high medical bill, inquire about payment plans or negotiate with the service provider. Look for discounts, promotions, or cheaper alternatives for necessary purchases.

5. Consider Available Resources: Assess if you have any available resources to help cover the expense. This could include using funds from your emergency fund, tapping into a savings account, or utilizing credit options if necessary. Be cautious with credit and use it responsibly to avoid accumulating excessive debt.

6. Prioritize Expenses: If you have multiple unexpected expenses, prioritize them based on urgency and importance. Address the most critical expenses first to prevent further financial hardship. Delay

non-essential expenses or find creative solutions to manage them within your means.

7. Seek Assistance: If the unexpected expense is overwhelming and you're struggling to manage it on your own, consider seeking assistance. Reach out to local community organizations, nonprofits, or government agencies that provide financial support or resources for individuals facing hardships.

8. Adjust Your Budget: After dealing with the unexpected expense, review and adjust your budget to accommodate any necessary changes. Take into account the impact of the expense on your overall financial situation and make the necessary adjustments to your savings goals or spending habits.

9. Learn from the Experience: Use the unexpected expense as an opportunity to learn and improve your financial preparedness. Assess what led to the unexpected expense and identify ways to prevent or minimize such situations in the future. Focus on building a more robust financial safety net to handle future emergencies.

Remember, unexpected expenses are a part of life, and while they can be stressful, being proactive and adaptable can help you navigate them more effectively. Building an emergency fund, maintaining a flexible budget, and seeking support when needed are key steps to handle unexpected expenses and maintain financial stability.

Coping With Lifestyle Inflation

Coping with lifestyle inflation, which refers to the tendency to increase spending as income increases, can be challenging but essential for long-term financial stability. Here are some strategies to help you manage lifestyle inflation:

1. Be Mindful and Aware: Recognize the tendency for lifestyle inflation and the potential negative impact it can have on your financial well-being. Understand that increased income doesn't necessarily mean you have to increase your expenses.

2. Set Financial Goals: Establish clear financial goals that align with your values and priorities. Whether it's saving for a down payment on a house, paying off debt, or investing for the future, having specific goals in mind can help you resist the urge to inflate your lifestyle unnecessarily.

3. Budget Wisely: Create a budget that reflects your financial goals and helps you allocate your income effectively. Be intentional about how you spend your money and prioritize essentials and savings over unnecessary expenses. Regularly review and adjust your budget to ensure it aligns with your changing financial situation.

4. Delay Gratification: Practice delayed gratification by resisting the urge to make immediate large purchases or indulge in extravagant spending. Instead, give yourself time to evaluate the necessity and long-term impact of the expense. Consider waiting before making big-ticket purchases to ensure they align with your financial goals.

5. Avoid Lifestyle Creep: Lifestyle creep occurs when your spending increases in proportion to your income without a corresponding increase in savings. Resist the temptation to upgrade your lifestyle every time you experience an increase in income. Maintain a modest and sustainable lifestyle that allows you to save and invest for the future.

6. Automate Savings and Investments: Set up automatic transfers to your savings and investment accounts. This ensures that a portion of your

income is saved or invested before you have the opportunity to spend it impulsively. Treat savings and investments as non-negotiable expenses.

7. Revisit Your Values: Reflect on what truly brings you fulfillment and happiness. Focus on experiences, relationships, and activities that align with your values rather than material possessions. Shifting your mindset can help you resist the temptation to inflate your lifestyle unnecessarily.

8. Be Selective with Increases: If you receive a raise or a higher-paying job, be mindful of how you allocate the extra income. Consider directing a significant portion towards savings, debt repayment, or investments rather than immediately increasing your spending.

9. Surround Yourself with Like-minded Individuals: Associate with people who share similar financial values and goals. Surrounding yourself with individuals who prioritize financial stability and prudent spending can help you stay accountable and resist the pressures of lifestyle inflation.

10. Regularly Assess Your Financial Progress: Review your financial situation regularly to track your progress towards your goals. Celebrate milestones and achievements along the way, but also remain aware of any signs of lifestyle inflation. Stay focused on your long-term financial well-being and make adjustments as necessary.

By being mindful, setting goals, budgeting wisely, and maintaining discipline, you can cope with lifestyle inflation and make intentional choices that lead to long-term financial success and stability. Remember, it's about finding a balance between enjoying your present life and securing your future.

Managing Budgeting Fatigue

Managing budget fatigue is important to stay motivated and committed to your financial goals. Here are some strategies to help you cope with budget fatigue:

1. Take Breaks: Allow yourself occasional breaks from budgeting. Taking short breaks can provide a mental and emotional reset, preventing burnout. Use this time to relax, engage in activities you enjoy, and rejuvenate yourself.

2. Celebrate Milestones: Recognize and celebrate the progress you've made in your financial journey. Set small milestones along the way and reward yourself when you achieve them. This can help maintain motivation and keep you focused on the bigger picture.

3. Find Support: Seek support from family, friends, or a community of like-minded individuals who are also committed to budgeting and financial goals. Discussing your challenges, sharing successes, and receiving encouragement can help you stay motivated and accountable.

4. Review and Adjust: Periodically review your budget and assess if it needs any adjustments. As circumstances change, your budget may need to be modified to better align with your current situation and goals. Flexibility in your budget can help alleviate some of the fatigue.

5. Explore New Strategies: If you find yourself getting bored or frustrated with your budgeting routine, try exploring new budgeting techniques or tools. There are various approaches available, such as the envelope system, 50/30/20 rule, or using budgeting apps. Experimenting with new methods can inject freshness and renewed enthusiasm into your budgeting process.

6. Focus on the Why: Remind yourself of the reasons why you started budgeting in the first place. Whether it's achieving financial freedom, paying off debt, or reaching specific goals, reconnecting with your underlying motivations can reignite your determination and help you push through the fatigue.

7. Seek Inspiration: Look for success stories, blogs, podcasts, or books about personal finance and budgeting. Hearing about others' journeys and how they overcame challenges can inspire and motivate you to keep going.

8. Practice Self-Care: Take care of yourself holistically, including your physical, mental, and emotional well-being. Engage in activities that help reduce stress and promote relaxation, such as exercise, meditation, hobbies, or spending time with loved ones. When you feel balanced and rejuvenated, it becomes easier to tackle budgeting challenges.

9. Visualize the Future: Visualize the financial goals you're working towards and imagine the positive impact achieving them will have on your life. This visualization can serve as a source of motivation and remind you of the long-term benefits of sticking to your budget.

10. Reflect on Progress: Reflect on how far you've come since you started budgeting. Review your financial achievements, such as paying off debt or increasing your savings. Acknowledging your progress can help rekindle your motivation and inspire you to keep pushing forward.

Remember that budgeting is a long-term commitment, and occasional fatigue is normal. By implementing these strategies, you can effectively manage budget fatigue and maintain your financial discipline, ultimately achieving your financial goals.

Chapter 10: Beyond Budgeting: Building Wealth

Building An Emergency Fund

Building an emergency fund is an important step towards financial security and preparedness. An emergency fund acts as a safety net to cover unexpected expenses or financial emergencies without relying on credit or incurring debt. Here are steps to help you build an emergency fund:

1. Set a Savings Goal: Determine how much you want to save for your emergency fund. A general guideline is to aim for three to six months' worth of living expenses. Consider your individual circumstances, such as income stability, financial obligations, and potential risks, to determine an appropriate savings target.

2. Calculate Your Expenses: Assess your monthly expenses, including essentials like rent/mortgage, utilities, groceries, transportation, insurance, and debt payments. Identify any discretionary expenses that can be temporarily reduced or eliminated to accelerate your savings.

3. Create a Budget: Develop a budget that aligns with your savings goal. Allocate a portion of your income specifically towards building your emergency fund. Treat this savings contribution as a non-negotiable expense, just like paying bills.

4. Automate Your Savings: Make saving for emergencies easier by setting up automatic transfers from your checking account to a dedicated savings account. Automating your savings ensures consistent progress and reduces the temptation to spend the funds elsewhere.

5. Start Small, Increase Over Time: If you're unable to save a significant amount initially, don't be discouraged. Start with a smaller savings goal and gradually increase it as you become more comfortable with saving and adjust your budget accordingly.

6. Cut Expenses and Increase Income: Look for opportunities to reduce your expenses and increase your income. Trim unnecessary costs, negotiate bills, or explore ways to earn additional income through side

gigs, freelancing, or part-time work. Redirect the savings and extra income towards your emergency fund.

7. Save Windfalls and Bonuses: When you receive unexpected money, such as tax refunds, bonuses, or monetary gifts, resist the urge to splurge. Instead, put a significant portion or the entire amount directly into your emergency fund to accelerate its growth.

8. Minimize Credit Card Reliance: As you build your emergency fund, try to minimize your reliance on credit cards for unexpected expenses. Relying on credit can lead to debt accumulation and hinder your progress. Having cash reserves in your emergency fund will provide a more sustainable solution.

9. Stay Disciplined: Stick to your budget and savings plan even when faced with temptations or setbacks. Remember the purpose and importance of your emergency fund, and remain committed to achieving your financial security.

10. Reassess and Replenish: If you have to dip into your emergency fund for unexpected expenses, make it a priority to replenish the fund as soon as possible. Adjust your budget and savings plan accordingly to restore the fund to its original target amount.

Building an emergency fund takes time and consistent effort, but it provides financial peace of mind and protects you from unexpected financial shocks. Stay focused on your savings goal, maintain discipline, and celebrate milestones along the way.

Saving For Retirement

Saving for retirement is a critical financial goal that requires long-term planning and consistent contributions. Here are steps to help you save for retirement:

1. Start Early: Time is a powerful ally when it comes to retirement savings. The earlier you start saving, the more time your money has to grow through compound interest. Even small contributions made over a long period can have a significant impact on your retirement nest egg.

2. Set a Retirement Goal: Determine the amount of money you'll need for a comfortable retirement. Consider factors such as your desired lifestyle, estimated expenses, healthcare costs, and inflation. Set a realistic goal to guide your savings efforts.

3. Calculate Retirement Savings Gap: Assess the gap between your projected retirement needs and your existing retirement savings. This will help you understand how much you need to save to reach your goal. Online retirement calculators or financial advisors can assist you in making these calculations.

4. Contribute to Employer-Sponsored Retirement Plans: If your employer offers a retirement plan, such as a 401(k) or 403(b), contribute to it. Take advantage of any matching contributions offered by your employer, as it's essentially free money that boosts your savings.

5. Individual Retirement Accounts (IRAs): Consider opening an IRA if you don't have access to an employer-sponsored retirement plan or want to supplement your savings. Traditional IRAs offer tax-deferred growth, while Roth IRAs provide tax-free withdrawals in retirement. Maximize your annual contributions to these accounts if possible.

6. Save Consistently: Set up automatic contributions to your retirement accounts. Consistency is key, as regular contributions allow your savings to grow steadily over time. Increase your contributions whenever possible, especially when you receive salary raises or bonuses.

7. Diversify Your Investments: Allocate your retirement savings across a diversified mix of investments, such as stocks, bonds, and mutual funds. Diversification helps spread risk and potentially increases returns. Consider your risk tolerance, time horizon, and consult with a financial advisor if needed.

8. Revisit and Adjust: Regularly review your retirement savings plan to ensure it remains on track. Reassess your retirement goals, adjust contributions as necessary, and rebalance your investment portfolio periodically to maintain an appropriate asset allocation.

9. Maximize Tax Advantages: Take advantage of any tax benefits associated with retirement savings. Contributions to certain retirement accounts may be tax-deductible (e.g., traditional 401(k) and traditional IRA), while others offer tax-free growth or withdrawals (e.g., Roth 401(k) and Roth IRA). Familiarize yourself with the tax rules and consult a tax professional for personalized advice.

10. Continuously Educate Yourself: Stay informed about retirement planning strategies, investment options, and changes in regulations. Attend seminars, read books, follow reputable financial websites, and seek advice from professionals. The more knowledge you have, the better equipped you'll be to make informed decisions about your retirement savings.

Remember that retirement savings is a long-term commitment, and it's essential to stay disciplined and consistent. Regularly monitor your progress, adjust your savings plan as needed, and consult with professionals to ensure you're on the right track. The earlier and more diligently you save for retirement, the greater the likelihood of enjoying a comfortable and financially secure retirement.

Growing Your Wealth Through Investments

Growing wealth through investments can be a valuable strategy to build long-term financial security. Here are some key points to consider:

1. Set Financial Goals: Clearly define your financial goals, such as saving for retirement, purchasing a home, or funding your children's education. Knowing your objectives will guide your investment decisions and time horizon.

2. Understand Risk and Return: Investments come with varying levels of risk and potential returns. Higher-risk investments, such as stocks, have the potential for greater returns but also carry more volatility. Lower-risk investments, like bonds or cash, offer more stability but may have lower returns. Assess your risk tolerance and determine the appropriate investment mix for your goals.

3. Diversify Your Portfolio: Diversification is important for managing risk. Spread your investments across different asset classes, such as stocks, bonds, real estate, and international markets. Within each asset class, diversify further by investing in various sectors or industries. Diversification helps mitigate the impact of any individual investment's performance on your overall portfolio.

4. Consider Investment Vehicles: Explore different investment vehicles based on your goals and risk tolerance. Some common options include stocks, bonds, mutual funds, exchange-traded funds (ETFs), real estate investment trusts (REITs), and index funds. Each has its own characteristics and benefits, so research and understand the specific features of each investment type.

5. Invest for the Long Term: Investing is a long-term endeavour. Time in the market allows your investments to benefit from compounding returns and ride out short-term market fluctuations. Avoid making impulsive investment decisions based on short-term

market movements and focus on the long-term performance of your portfolio.

6. Conduct Research: Thoroughly research investment opportunities before committing your capital. Analyze financial statements, market trends, and company fundamentals for individual stocks. For funds and other investments, review performance history, expense ratios, and fund managers' expertise. Stay informed about economic indicators and global events that can impact markets.

7. Dollar-Cost Averaging: Consider using dollar-cost averaging as an investment strategy. Instead of investing a lump sum, regularly invest a fixed amount over time, regardless of market conditions. This approach reduces the impact of market volatility on your investments and allows you to buy more shares when prices are low.

8. Rebalance Your Portfolio: Periodically review and rebalance your portfolio to ensure it aligns with your target asset allocation. Over time, some investments may outperform while others may underperform. Rebalancing involves selling over-performing assets and buying underperforming ones to maintain your desired asset mix.

9. Seek Professional Advice: If you're unsure about investment strategies or lack the time to manage your portfolio, consider working with a financial advisor. They can provide personalized advice based on your goals, risk tolerance, and financial situation.

10. Stay Informed and Be Patient: Stay updated on market trends, economic indicators, and changes in investment regulations. However, avoid making hasty investment decisions based on short-term news or market fluctuations. Patience is key in investing, and maintaining a long-term perspective is essential.

Remember that investing involves risks, and there are no guarantees of returns. It's important to do your due diligence, diversify your investments, and monitor your portfolio regularly. Be prepared for market fluctuations and consult with financial professionals when needed. Over time, disciplined investing and a well-constructed portfolio have the potential to grow your wealth and help you achieve your financial goals.

Conclusion:

Congratulations! You've completed "Mastering Your Finances: A Guide to Budgeting." By implementing the techniques and strategies outlined in this book, you have taken the first steps toward financial empowerment. Remember, budgeting is a continuous process that requires discipline and regular review. With practice, you will become more proficient at managing your money, achieving your financial goals, and securing a brighter future. Good luck on your financial journey!

www.ingramcontent.com/pod-product-compliance
Lightning Source LLC
LaVergne TN
LVHW090427210926
848480LV00002B/725